# SCIENCE FACT OR FICTION?
## YOU DECIDE!

Sarah Levete

# Crabtree Publishing Company
## www.crabtreebooks.com

**Author:** Sarah Levete
**Editor:** Kathy Middleton
**Production coordinator:** Ken Wright
**Prepress technician:** Margaret Amy Salter
**Series consultant:** Gill Matthews

**Picture Credits:**
CERN: Maximilien Brice 13
Istockphoto: Joze Pojbic 5, 15, 28t,
    Richvintage 11b, Xyno 21t
NASA: 12, JPL/USGS 14l
Rex Features/Sipa Press 23, SNAP 16l, 20t
Shutterstock: (Cover) Gary Blakeley 9, Stephen
    Coburn 19r, Petronilo G. Dangoy Jr. 27b, Farawaykid
    14r, Stephen Finn 24b, Benjamin Albiach Galan 28b,
    Sebastian Kaulitzki 8–9, Kenishirotie 27t, Kirsanov
    11t, Zastol`skiy Victor Leonidovich 24t, Theodore
    Littleton 17, Piotr Marcinski 4l, Mark R 8, Andreas
    Meyer 4–32, 10, Yannis Ntousiopoulos 4r, Tyler
    Olson 25br, Tyler Penler 19l, Glenda M. Powers 25b,
    Lee Prince 18, Sudheer Sakthan 25t, 29c, Jozef
    Sedmak 6, Mark Stout Photography 26-27, 29b,
    Marek Szumlas 7b, Miroslav Tolimir 20-21, Ismael
    Montero Verdu 7t, Paul Vorwerk 22, 29t

Every effort has been made to trace copyright holders and to obtain their permission for use of copyright material. The authors and publishers would be pleased to rectify any error or omission in future editions. All the Internet addresses given in this book were correct at the time of going to press. The author and publishers regret any inconvenience caused if addresses have changed or sites have ceased to exist, but can accept no responsibility for any such changes.

**Library and Archives Canada Cataloguing in Publication**

Levete, Sarah
    Science fact or fiction? : you decide! / Sarah Levete.

(Crabtree connections)
Includes index.
ISBN 978-0-7787-9895-8 (bound).--ISBN 978-0-7787-9916-0 (pbk.)

    1. Science--Miscellanea--Juvenile literature. 2. Curiosities and wonders--Juvenile literature. I. Title. II. Series: Crabtree connections

Q163.L475 2010          j502          C2010-905073-8

**Library of Congress Cataloging-in-Publication Data**

Levete, Sarah.
    Science fact or fiction? : you decide! / Sarah Levete.
        p. cm. -- (Crabtree connections)
    Includes index.
    ISBN 978-0-7787-9916-0 (pbk. : alk. paper) -- ISBN 978-0-7787-9895-8 (reinforced library binding : alk. paper)
    1. Science--Juvenile literature. 2. Science fiction--Juvenile literature. I. Title. II. Series.

Q163L43 2011
500--dc22

                                                    2010030823

Printed in the U.S.A./082010/WO20101210

**Published in Canada**
**Crabtree Publishing**
616 Welland Ave.
St. Catharines, Ontario
L2M 5V6

**Published in the United States**
**Crabtree Publishing**
PMB 59051
350 Fifth Avenue, 59th Floor
New York, New York 10118

# Contents

# True or False?

**Aliens** coming to Earth?
Dinosaurs walking the streets?
Not everything you read
is true! Not everything
you are told is true.
It can be very hard
to know what
to believe.

*Could dinosaurs
walk on Earth
again?*

*Will robots rule
the world?*

ANGER

HATE

HAPPINESS

OPTIMISM

ATE

FRUSTRATION

HOPE

LOVE

PESSIMISM

PLEASURE

SADNESS

## True or false?

Scientists have discovered many amazing things about our world. They can explain some of these things, and prove that they are real. Other things are much harder to prove, and no one knows for sure if they exist or not.

## You decide

On the next pages, you will read about many incredible events and ideas. Are any of these real, or are they just made-up stories? It's up to you to decide whether what you have read is true, false, or unknown. Then check out the answers on pages 28 and 29.

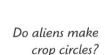

*Do aliens make crop circles?*

# Will Dinosaurs Live Again?

You know, of course, that dinosaurs died out over 65 million years ago. But did you also know that they might come back to life and walk around our streets? Read on to find out more.

Jurassic Park *is a **fictional** film about dinosaurs brought back to life by scientists. But could it really happen?*

## DNA to Dinosaur

Scientists have made **clones**, or copies, of sheep and cows from their **DNA**. This is the material inside a living thing that controls what it looks like and what it does.

If scientists can do this, why can't they make a copy of a dinosaur from dinosaur DNA? All they have to do is get DNA from a fossil or bone. Do you think dinosaurs will walk on Earth again?

Dinosaur bones contain DNA.

Could dinosaurs run wild on Earth once more?

### FOR REAL

**CLOSE RELATIVES**
*Birds and lizards are closely related to dinosaurs. They might even contain some of the DNA that will help scientists recreate dinosaurs.*

True ☐ False ☐ Unknown ☐

# The Bermuda Triangle

In an area of the Atlantic Ocean known as the Bermuda Triangle, planes and ships have vanished without a trace, never to be seen again.

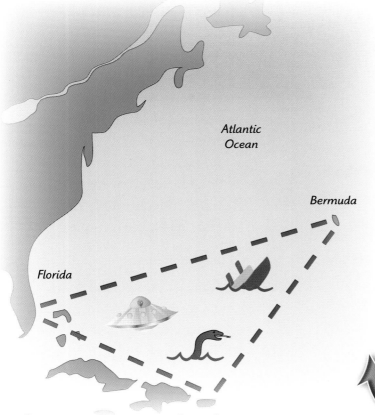

Atlantic Ocean

Florida

Bermuda

Puerto Rico

## What happened?

Maybe this is the work of some mysterious, **supernatural** force. Strange as it sounds, it might be true. But some people refuse to believe this. They blame the vanishings on bad weather and other causes.

*There have been many reports of ships and planes vanishing in the Bermuda Triangle.*

Before the planes lost radio contact, a crew member said, "Everything looks strange, even the ocean."

## Does this explain it?
Some people say sudden storms cause ships and planes to disappear or that it's the **crew's** fault. Possibly. But if this is true, wouldn't we see more **evidence**? When a plane crashes in bad weather or a ship sinks, wreckage scatters everywhere. Yet, nothing is ever left behind in the Bermuda Triangle.

That leaves only one possible explanation—it really is the work of some mysterious, unknown supernatural force that controls the Bermuda Triangle. Right?

## FOR REAL

### DISAPPEARING PLANES
In 1945, five American army planes were on an everyday **mission**. The weather was calm, and the planes were in good condition. But the pilots and crew were never seen or heard from again. Two rescue planes flew out to find the others. They also disappeared. No one has ever found any **wreckage** from the seven planes.

True ☐  False ☐  Unknown ☐

# Bigfoot on the Loose?

Do you believe in monsters? Maybe you should. There are many reports of strange creatures, half human and half ape, roaming through forests around the world. From North America to Southeast Asia, people have reported seeing heavy, hairy creatures. But these creatures aren't tall apes, hairy humans, or bears. They're monsters!

*This artist's drawing is based on sightings of Bigfoot. It shows what the monster may look like.*

## The facts

No one has captured this monster, but they have found hair from its body and seen its mighty footprints in snow on mountains and in mud in jungles.

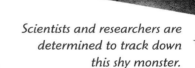

*Scientists and researchers are determined to track down this shy monster.*

*Could this be Bigfoot captured on film, or is it a hoax?*

## Giant footprints

Bigfoot was first seen in Tibet in 1832. Since then many people claim to have seen its footprints, which are too big to belong to a known animal or a human.

### FOR REAL

Scientists have carried out tests on strands of Bigfoot's hair to see if its DNA matches that of any other known creature. It doesn't. Are we dealing with a monster?

True ☐ False ☐ Unknown ☐

# Can You Travel Through Time?

When you look up at the bright stars on a clear night, you are looking at light that existed millions of years ago. You are looking into the past. If you can look into the past, why can't you travel there? Well, maybe you can.

black hole

spacecraft

*Could we travel through a black hole in a spacecraft like this?*

### Black holes of time

When a star reaches the end of its life, it breaks down and forms a **black hole**. The **gravity** in this hole sucks in everything around it. Scientists think that there are tunnels called wormholes that link black holes together. These are like passageways through time. Could we use these wormholes to travel through time?

# Traveling through black holes

Some scientists think they can make a spacecraft that can travel through a black hole so that we'll be able to travel through time. Perhaps one day we will all be time travelers.

Black holes are just one of the things scientists hope to explain by using the Large Hadron Collider (LHC) machine. The LHC is a super machine being used to recreate what the universe was like after the Big Bang.

True ☐   False ☐   Unknown ☐

# Are Aliens Real?

Hundreds of people say they have met **aliens**. Many people have reported seeing strange glowing lights in the sky. These people could be telling the truth, even if others don't believe them...

Aliens could be living on Mars.

## Life on Mars

Scientists have found evidence of water on Mars. Living things need water. These signs of water mean there may be life on Mars. Could aliens be there, too?

## Crop circles

Crop circles are amazing shapes cut into farmers' fields— overnight. No one ever sees anything or anybody making the shapes. Could aliens have made them?

*This strange shape appeared overnight in a field in England. What else, other than aliens, could have made it?*

### STRANGE HAPPENINGS IN ROSWELL

*In 1947, people in a town called Roswell in New Mexico found strange wreckage in the desert. They said they saw bodies of odd creatures, which looked like aliens. The local people believed it was the wreckage of an alien spaceship.*

## What other explanation?

Can you find a better explanation for glowing lights and strange events? If you can't, perhaps you should consider that aliens are real!

True ☐ False ☐ Unknown ☐

# Can Robots Rule?

It would be pretty cool to have a robot that cleans your room or does your homework. At the moment, robots do what humans tell them to, and that's great. But will there be problems if we make robots that are smarter than us? If you don't think robots could rule the world, read on.

*In the film* The Terminator, *robots rule the world.*

## Progress

Fifty years ago, a robot could only lift an arm. Today, robots cook and clean. Some show feelings and think. In fifty years, robots will be even smarter than humans. Will we end up working for them?

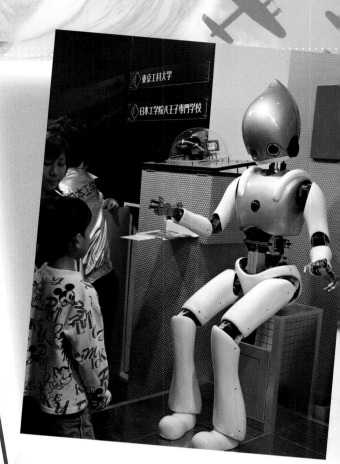

## FOR REAL

**ALREADY THINKING**

*In 2002, a robot called Gaak was on **display** at a science show in England. But Gaak sneaked away. The owners of the runaway robot finally caught it hiding near the highway! Gaak was thinking and behaving independently. What's to stop robots in the future from ruling the world?*

*Could robots one day teach children, too?*

**True** ☐ **False** ☐ **Unknown** ☐

# Does Lightning Strike Twice?

During a loud thunderstorm, flashes of lightning zigzag across the stormy sky. Sometimes, but not often, those lightning flashes crash to the ground. Sometimes the lightning will strike tall buildings, trees, and even people. And sometimes lightning even strikes twice—although some people will tell you it doesn't.

## FOR REAL

### HOT, WHITE ELECTRICITY

*Lightning is made by electrical charges in a storm cloud. Each year, lightning injures about 100,000 people in the world and kills about 10,000.*

*This huge spark of electricity is about six times hotter than the Sun.*

*The Sun is boiling hot, but lightning is even hotter.*

## What are the chances?

Scientists say you have a one in 5,000 chance of being struck by lightning. And you have a one in 9 million chance of being struck by lightning twice. Are the odds against it happening really too high?

*The Empire State Building in New York is hit by lightning about 25 times a year.*

**True** ☐ **False** ☐ **Unknown** ☐

# Atlantis: Island Under the Sea

About 3,500 years ago, there was an island called Atlantis. The people who lived on the island were very rich and powerful. Then suddenly, this bustling place sank to the bottom of the ocean and disappeared completely!

## Can an island sink?

Some people think the Atlantis tale is true! But surely no reasonable person can believe it's possible for an island to sink without a trace?

*The story of Atlantis may not be true, but it is still a great idea for a fictional film.*

## Spreading rumors

About 2,300 years ago, an ancient Roman writer called Plato talked about a huge wave swallowing up an island. This is how the story of Atlantis began.

We know that fierce floods and earthquakes can destroy towns, and cities, but there is usually some wreckage left from the disaster. There is none from Atlantis. So if it ever existed, where's the evidence?

*Plato's writings about a lost island began the myth of Atlantis.*

*Some people believe that the island of Santorini in Greece, partly sunken after a volcanic explosion, may once have been Atlantis.*

True ☐ False ☐ Unknown ☐

# Is There a Mummy's Curse?

**Archaeologists** have discovered lots of information about ancient Egyptians and their lives. But in digging up the past, they may have also dug up the deadly **mummy's curse**!

## Boy king dies!

An ancient Egyptian boy king called Tutankhamun died over 3,000 years ago. He was buried in a **tomb** with incredible riches. In 1922, the archaeologist Howard Carter broke into the tomb.

*Carter discovered treasures such as Tutankhamun's gold burial mask. Was this discovery worth releasing the mummy's curse?*

When Carter entered the tomb, a cobra inside ate his pet canary. In ancient Egyptian belief, the cobra protected the **pharaoh**.

## The Curse

A sign inside warned that anyone who disturbed Tutankhamun's burial place would be cursed. Carter and his friends ignored the warning. Read what happened to them below.

### FOR REAL

### CURSE OR COINCIDENCE?

■ A man called Carnarvon, who paid for Carter's work, died suddenly. At exactly the same time, his dog also died, and all the lights went out in the busy Egyptian city of Cairo.

■ Many of the men who entered the tomb died at a young age. How can this be explained?

True ☐  False ☐  Unknown ☐

23

# Can You Fly in a Tornado?

Everyone knows that birds can fly, but did you know that cats, dogs, fish, and cows have been seen in the air too? It's hard to believe, but it's true!

## How it happens

A fierce and violent wind called a **tornado** forms a **funnel** like a spinning top, which whizzes around at an incredible 250 miles (400 km) per hour. As it spins, the tornado sucks up anything on the ground, including animals.

*These heavy cars and ships were picked up by a tornado, then dropped back onto the ground.*

### FOR REAL

### FLYING COWS

*In 1949 in Oklahoma, a farmer saw 12 of his cows carried away in a tornado. They tumbled and rolled in the whirling wind before the terrified animals dropped into a far away field. Incredibly, they survived! Do you think humans could be swept into the air by a tornado, too?*

True ☐ False ☐ Unknown ☐

# Water Puzzle

Does water really go down the drain in different directions in Australia and North America?

*In which direction does water swirl down a drain? It depends where you live in the world.*

## In a spin

Watch water run down a drain. Does it swirl from left to right, or right to left? If you ask someone in Australia, they will say it disappears in the opposite direction that it does here. In the northern **hemisphere**, water drains counterclockwise; in the southern hemisphere it drains clockwise.

## FOR REAL

### A WINDY EXPLANATION

*The Earth completes one **rotation** every 24 hours. As it spins, it pulls the winds in the north to the right and the winds in the south to the left. This is called the Coriolis Effect. It is this strong pull that controls the direction of the water as it flows down a drain. It pulls the water either to the right or the left, depending on where you live in the world.*

## Nonbelievers

Some people say that just because the Earth spins around, it doesn't affect the way in which water goes down a drain. They say this is impossible and a silly idea. What do you believe?

*Does water swirl counterclockwise in North America?*

*Does water swirl clockwise in Australia?*

True ☐ False ☐ Unknown ☐

# The Facts

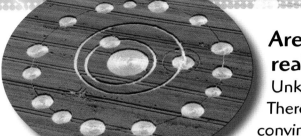

## Will dinosaurs live again?
False! There is not enough DNA around to recreate a living dinosaur.

## Are aliens real?
Unknown! There is still no convincing scientific evidence to date.

## The Bermuda Triangle
Unknown! No proof exists of supernatural forces.

## Can robots rule?
False! Robots cannot organize themselves or **reproduce**.

## Bigfoot on the loose?
Unknown! No evidence to date proves its existence.

## Does lightning strike twice?
True! Lightning strikes by chance, but it has been documented to have hit the same person, place, or thing more than one time.

## Can you travel through time?
False! No one's figured out how—yet!

## Atlantis: an island beneath the sea
Unknown! No evidence has yet been found.

## Is there really a curse of the mummy?
Unknown! All the bad luck could have just been coincidences.

## Can a human really fly in a tornado?
True! Tornadoes sometimes pick up the people, cars, and animals in their path and then drop them down.

## Water puzzle?
False! There is no convincing scientific proof.

# Glossary

**archaeologist** A person who studies history by looking at objects found from the past

**alien** Not belonging to planet Earth

**black hole** An invisible body in space which pulls objects toward it because of very strong gravity

**clone** An exact copy of a creature made using its DNA

**crew** People who work on a ship or plane

**curse** An unlucky spell

**display** On show

**DNA** Material that contains a code that controls what a living thing looks like

**evidence** Proof

**fictional** Made up

**funnel** A shape like a narrow tube

**gravity** Earth's natural pulling force that makes objects fall downward

**hemisphere** Northern or southern part of the world

**mission** A specific task

**mummy** A dead body that is wrapped up in special bandages to stop it decaying

**pharaoh** An ancient Egyptian king

**reproduce** Make more

**rotation** One complete turn of 360 degrees

**supernatural** A force for which there is no scientific or reasonable explanation

**tomb** A place where someone is buried

**tornado** A violent wind that sucks up objects in its path

**wreckage** Remains after a disaster

# Further Information

## Web Sites

The Bermuda Triangle
**www.kidzworld.com/article/
1136-scary-places-4-the-
bermuda-triangle**

Atlantis
**www.kidzworld.com/article/
960-history-the-lost-city-
of-atlantis**

Tornadoes
**http://skydiary.com/kids/
tornadoes.html**

Lightning
**www.ucar.edu/communications/
infopack/lightning/kids.html**

Mummy's Curse
**http://egypt.mrdonn.org/
mummycurse.html**

Bigfoot
**www.kidzworld.com/
article/2220-the-legends-of-
bigfoot-sasquatch-and-the-yeti**

Dinosaurs
**www.sdnhm.org/research/
paleontology/jp_qanda.html**

Robots
**www.thetech.org/robotics/
ethics/index.html**

Aliens
**www.roswellufomuseum.com/
incident.htm**

Black Holes
**http://spaceplace.nasa.gov/en/
kids/blackhole/index.shtml**

Water Down the Drain
**www.weatherimagery.com/blog/
water-spin-down-drain/**

# Index